THE
Archive Photographs
SERIES
DOWNHAM MARKET

Compiled by
Mike Bullen

CHALFORD

First published 1998
Copyright © Mike Bullen, 1998

The Chalford Publishing Company
St Mary's Mill, Chalford,
Stroud, Gloucestershire, GL6 8NX

ISBN 0 7524 1093 8

Typesetting and origination by
The Chalford Publishing Company
Printed in Great Britain by
Bailey Print, Dursley, Gloucestershire

Contents

TOWN CLOCK, the symbol of the town. It was presented by Mr James Scott, esq., to the town in 1878 at a cost of £450. The picture shows T.R. Smith's grocers shop in the background, which is now a fish and chip shop.

Introduction

This book is an attempt to convey in words and pictures some of the changes that have occurred in Downham Market and the three villages south of the town. The book has drawn on my own large collection of postcards and photographs acquired during twelve years of collecting and research. Over a number of years of conducting town walks and displays during the Downham Market Festival week, I have often been asked 'why aren't you writing a book', so, over the last few months I have been doing just that; choosing the pictures to be included and collecting the information for the captions to accompany each one.

I have attempted to show as many facets of the town and village life as I can. Many of these pictures were taken early this century by amateur and professional photographers who have left a unique pictorial legacy of a bygone age, which remained largely unchanged until the arrival of the motor car when streets, roads and buildings were altered for ever. Early this century, before mass travel, people sent postcards with messages to friends and relatives, often building up collections which have survived to the present day and have been handed down. Unfortunately, many postcards have also been destroyed or lost over the years thus depriving us of a great deal of visual, and anecdotal, knowledge.

Downham has been a shopping focal point, with its Friday market, for many years, with people travelling into town from some of the villages that are also featured in this book. First they came by cart, then by bus or car, buying their weekly requirements and coming to know Downham well. My grateful thanks go to the many people both in the town and the villages who have given me their time and allowed me to copy pictures and record information, enabling me to compile this first pictorial history of the area.

My special thanks go to my wife Wendy for her patience and to my daughters; Emma for proof reading and helping with the layout and Catherine for keeping me going!

One

Downham Market

Dowham Market was originally called Dunham or Duneham (ham being Anglo-Saxon for town). Dun or Down means hill and 'town on a hill' is an apt description. Edward the Confessor granted the town market status in around 900 A.D., thus confirming its right to hold a weekly market. Although it was originally held on Saturdays, the present day market is now held on Fridays and Saturdays.

Built on Ackerman Way, an old Roman road, Downham's prominent position overlooking the fens and beside the River Great Ouse has made it ideally suited for ease of trade over many centuries. Large quantities of butter bought up river, were sold at market in Downham each year (90,000 firkins or 2,250 tons, at one time), then transported again by river, to Cambridge as 'Cambridge butter'. By the early 1850s this market was obsolete and trade in corn, wool and cattle replaced it, being more suited to the area.

Among Downham Market's claims to fame are, firstly, that Nelson spent some of his days at school in Bridge Street, and, secondly, that Charles I stayed three days at The White Swan after his defeat at the Battle of Naseby.

DOWNHAM RAILWAY STATION, *c.*1907, was officially opened on 27 October 1846. The picture shows Mr George Hewitt (centre) going on his first train journey to Cambridge.

AERIAL VIEW, showing St John's Eau (now Relief Channel) in the foreground. The Hythe and Great Ouse tidal river is pictured at the top.

100   Bridge Road, Downham   Photo Raby

THE HYTHE, Downham West, c.1930. Coal was brought up river on a barge and at high tide off-loaded into the warehouses behind.

10,934   Old Stone Bridge, Downham Market.

STONE BRIDGE, over St John's Eau river. It was demolished in the early 1960s to make way for the 'Flood Relief Channel' bridge.

98   Bridge Road and Mill, Downham   Photo Raby

MAIDEN'S WALK, with Eagles Mill in the background. It is now Heygates Mill.

BRIDGE STREET (1906), showing how people had time to stop to have their photographs taken. The cobbles were removed in 1925.

Bridge Street Downham.

BRIDGE STREET, c. 1930. 'Granny' Roger's sweet shop is situated on the right of the picture. Around this time Downham's first telephone exchange was operated from what had been the largest public house, The Queens Head, hence young Victoria's head over the door to the left of the picture.

BRIDGE STREET, 1907, showing the Quaker meeting house (now the library). A small boy (third from left) is carrying two buckets on a yoke presumably fetching or carrying water from the pump on the Green.

THE MARKET HOUSE public house. This picture was taken from a passing motor cycle. The building was converted into a fish and chip shop before its demolition and the area made into a car park.

MARKET PLACE, c. 1885. Ellen Emery's shop, is being prepared for demolition. It was replaced by the Town Hall. Emery's moved to 21 Bridge Street to continue selling 'London's latest fashions'. Their mannequin parades attracted 300-400 people into the new Town Hall for an evening's entertainment.

MARKET PLACE, c. 1906, showing the clock, town pump and the new Town Hall having been built in 1887 at a cost of £1,700. The foundation stone was laid on 29 October 1887, by William Amhurst Tyssen Ammerst, MP. It was refurbished during 1934 and extended in 1974.

MARKET PLACE, c. 1960. The Pagoda was erected in place of the town pump in 1936. It comprised toilets, a drinking fountain and telephone kiosk. It was demolished 27 years later in 1965.

TOWN PUMP, Market Place. The pump was removed to the Howdale in 1935 by J. Long & Son, the stonemasons. It was one of four pumps around town. Station Road, Lynn Road and London Road were the sites of the other three.

HIGH STREET, *c.*1922. The land between Bayfield's butchers shop (later Bowman's) and Leopold Peter's shop (later Parrott's) was gardens until approximately 1935 when two shops were built. The Chequers public house is in the background.

HIGH STREET, 1907. There were few changes made to the High Street until the 1960s when plate-glass windows for displaying shops' wares required the removal of all small doors and windows. Dormer windows have replaced the top floor of the three storey building.

16

CASTLE HOTEL, 11 January 1907. One of Downham's two coaching inns pictured after a heavy snow fall. Even then people could wait to have their photographs taken.

CASTLE YARD, c. 1920. It used to be covered over, allowing the horses to be prepared for sale away from the elements. Only two supports from the original building remain.

LONDON ROAD, *c.*1925, with Johnny Long's stonemason's show room which was demolished in 1965. The washeteria is now situated next door.

THE CHAMBERS, *c.*1880, London Road with Zacaria Vince, cart and jig makers. Their saw pit for cutting cart shafts used to be situated where the war memorial once stood. The site is now occupied by a washeteria.

THE WORKHOUSE (UNION), designed by W.J. Donthorne. It was built in 1836, in Tudor-style and constructed of white brick and carstone, costing all of £5,000. It was renamed The Union when it became an old people's home with about 200-250 residents. In 1967 it was demolished when it became too expensive to repair.

STAFF of The Union posing outside its grand entrance, c.1960.

SALAMANCA HOUSE, 1913. One of Downham's oldest houses built in 1810, it is named after the famous battle of Salamanca of 1812. When the owner died in about 1898 it was divided into two halves, one being left to the butler and the other to the maid.

DOWNHAM ROAD DENVER, c. 1910, viewed looking back into Downham from outside Crow Hall. Bungalows now stand on much of the parkland. Jim Russell's garage stands on the bend in the middle distance.

Crow Hall, Downham

Valentine's Series

CROW HALL, August 1904. For the first half of this century, Crow Hall was run as a private school, Mr and Mrs Page being the last owners. During the war it was requisitioned for the land army. In the 1960s it became a family commune.

LONDON ROAD, 1955, looking towards Downham. Jim Russell's garage now occupies the road frontage with the entrance to Park Lane situated were the gate used to be.

PARADISE ROAD was the 'road to Paradise'. Formerly Parsons Lane, it was renamed because of the gallows sited on this road. Pictured is the The Castle Tap public house. Shooting parties would meet at the Castle Hotel, where the gentry would drink while their servants were sent to drink in The Tap.

SILENT CINEMA, Paradise Road. Built in 1913, it was run by Mr Chadwick, a photographer and postcard seller. It closed during 1934 and the premises were used as Lovell's car showroom until its demolition in December 1983.

PRIORY TERRACE, before the war. These ornate railings were removed during the war 'to help the war effort'. It is believed that most of the iron work removed in the town only got as far as Lynn docks, where it remained until the war ended.

HILL HOUSE SCHOOL, Bridge Street. Mrs Markam, the principal, advertised in the 1920s to 'undertake to teach pupils fifteen years of age, whose parents desire it, entire household management, with special attention paid to the physical well-being of the pupil'.

POST OFFICE, *c.*1955. General view showing relative positions of buildings in the following pictures. Only the post office (centre) and the right hand side building remain.

PRIMITIVE METHODIST CHAPEL, London Road. Built in 1871 at a cost of £1,055, it had seating for 400 people. The year 1874 saw the addition of a minister's house to the chapel grounds. After the combined Methodist Chapel was opened in Paradise Road on 16 July 1966, the Primitive Chapel was demolished.

WAR MEMORIAL dedicated in 1924. Behind the memorial Johnny Long's stonemasons occupied the junction between Church and London Road. The premises were demolished during road improvements in 1965.

WAR MEMORIAL, London Road. Ken Russell used to run a watch repair business from the small building behind the memorial.

ST EDMUND'S CHURCH INTERIOR before the rood screen and pulpit were erected in 1912.

CHURCH AVENUE (1908). This avenue of beech trees existed until 1966 when the town centre bypass was built. 'The Great Wall of Downham' (as it was nicknamed) required the removal of the left hand row of trees. The iron gates were removed to help the war effort.

SOUNDING ALLEY, *c.*1919. In the 1700s a Mr Osborn ran a bell foundry beside the alley, hence its name. Bells cast in Downham are still being rung in some Pacific island churches to this day.

STANNARD'S bakery stood on Cannon Square, formerly Hogg Hill. It was also known as Valance and later as Scotts. Along with various houses it helped to support the church foundations. The need for road improvements led to their demolition in 1965.

LYNN ROAD, looking into town. Every building was demolished except the large house on the extreme left of the picture for the road to be straightened.

CHEQUERS INN, Lynn Road. This public house was demolished in 1965 along with Hunter's shoe shop, Marriott's harness makers, Andrew's garage and two rows of cottages.

LYNN ROAD, 1911. Hawkin's offices and cottages on the left remain the same today. Andrew's garage and cottages on the right were demolished in 1965.

LYNN ROAD. Downham's only fireworks factory was situated in buildings between the cottages.

Red Cross Hospital, Tower House, Downham

THE TOWERS, originally the home of Mr James Scott. During the First World War it was used as a military hospital and afterwards as a home for the mentally handicapped. A fire that began on August Bank Holiday 1966 destroyed the whole building.

F. H. Chadwick. Downham

TOWERS' HOSPITAL STAFF photographed outside the main door in 1917.

The Howdale, Downham

THE HOWDALE, *c.* 1910, covering approximately 7 acres. It was left to the town 'for the enjoyment of the townsfolk' by, it is believed, two ladies: a Mrs How and a Mrs Dale.

AERIEL VIEW, *c.* 1930, looking east. The long building on the middle left of the picture was a malt house. Last used in about 1955, it is now the site of Somerfield supermarket.

31

New Secondary School, Downham.

(Photo Raby)

SECONDARY SCHOOL, Ryston End. It was opened on 20 May 1931 by Major E.H. Evans-Lombe, after he was presented with a key by Mr E.H. Birch, Chairman of Governers. It was built in the grounds of a grand country house dating back to the seventeenth century. It has since been a Grammar School and now provides for Year 7 and for the Sixth Form.

Lovers Walk Down.

RYSTON END, c. 1930. It was formerly known as Lover's Lane before the development of private houses began on the right hand side.

Downham Rectory.

RECTORY, *c.* 1910, built on the site of a Benedictine monastery. In October 1958 this 3 acre site was sold for £3,350 and became Downham's Rural District Council offices, which still stand.

The Rectory, Downham   41479

RECTORY; rear view showing part of the well maintained gardens. Council garages now occupy this land.

BRIDGE ROAD, 1930.

IRON BRIDGE, opened in February 1879 and cost £3,500. This iron lattice bridge was supported on two sets of pillars. It was replaced in 1964 with the present one costing £75,000.

Two
Trade

Over the years numerous shops have been demolished or have changed hands many times. Some, like Laxons, bring back memories of freshly ground coffee and of watching your money disappear in a holder suspended by wire, which winged its way down to the cashier and returned with your change, while you sat beside a polished wooden counter. How times have changed.

CASH & Co's Market Place shop with Mr Bryan and staff.

CASH & Co. (Avertising card), 1920s. I particularly like their 'Snowdrop' and 'Hyacinth' brand names for stylish footwear.

A. POPE'S furnishers shop, *c.* 1907, advertising their 'Great Furnishing Store', selling carpets, bedsteads and general ironmongery. Mr Pope sold up in 1912, advertising in the *Downham Gazette & Journal* on 30 March 1912 a 'compulsory sale'. It was demolished by November 1915 and replaced by Whitehead's butchers shop. 1969 saw Whitehead's and Gunn's furnishers next-door demolished to make way for A.T. Johnsons.

MR TOMMY WHITEHEAD showing off his prize winning bull, which would have been paraded around town before its slaughter.

WADE-WRIGHTS ice creams. Their motto was 'Stop me and buy one'. Ice creams would be delivered to the town and surrounding villages from the Priory Road factory.

AMOS BARBER TIN WARE MANUFACTURERS (1924). Mr Barber manufactured pots and pans etc. for troops during the First World War. Opposite were the ovens, furnace and stove enamelling workshops. Mr Harry Hewitt is controlling the horse. The premises later became Wade-Wright's ice cream factory. When it was Downham Engineering Company's premises it was extended and had a new fascia added.

LAXON'S delivery lorry, *c.*1919. It was presumably surplus from the war. Note the telephone number 1.

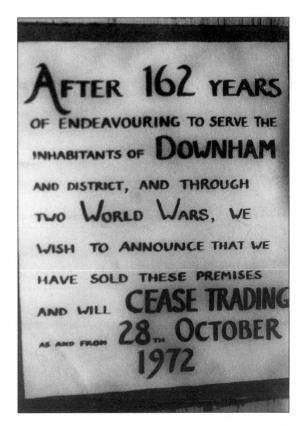

AFTER 162 YEARS OF ENDEAVOURING TO SERVE THE INHABITANTS OF DOWNHAM AND DISTRICT, AND THROUGH TWO WORLD WARS, WE WISH TO ANNOUNCE THAT WE HAVE SOLD THESE PREMISES AND WILL CEASE TRADING AS AND FROM 28TH OCTOBER 1972

LAXON'S, High Street. The sign is announcing their closure.

BLACKSMITH'S SHOP, Railway Road, *c.* 1925. This has now been converted into a private dwelling.

'I WANT YOUR WORK' proclaims the sign outside Bunkall harness maker's premises in Bridge Street, *c.* 1912.

SHERWOOD'S MOTOR CYCLE business 22 March 1929 in Paradise Road. Lou Sherwood sits astride a B.S.A., with his father (left) looking on.

LINGLEY & SYMMONDS, grocers at 16 Bridge Street. Here they are advertising their Christmas stock and winning first prize for their window display. Mr Harry Wright took over the shop as a going concern.

HARRY REED, Station Road, c.1908. Mr Harry Reed stands proudly outside his shop, before it moved to its current premises in Bridge Street.

ELLEN EMERY'S shop at 21 Bridge Street. It was later given telephone No. 2 after her move from the Market Place.

MASTIN'S 'HYGIENIC BAKERY', High Street. The cardboard wedding cake was on display for many years. On Christmas Day, Mr Mastin would use the bread ovens to roast customers' poultry.

INTERNATIONAL STORES' delivery horse and cart (1924), with Mr Bert Batson of Ten Mile Bank. The horse was hired from Mr R. Raby, on whose field this photograph was taken.

HERBERT RABY'S SHOP (The fancy bazaar), 39 Bridge Street. Herbert Raby was a postcard publisher, photographer and seller of a wide range of goods including china, picture frames, music, gramophones and records.

LEOPOLD PETER'S 'THE CORSET HOUSE', Cannon Square/High Street, c. 1920. This was just one of many ladies fashion shops in the town.

MR AND MRS HUNTER standing outside their shoe shop in Lynn Road.

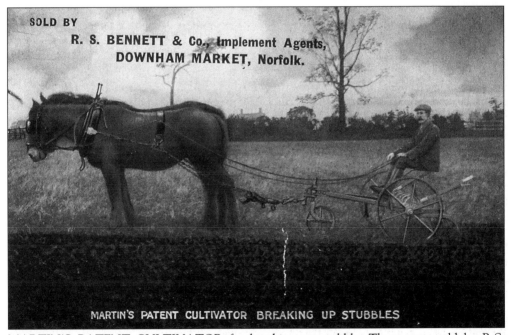

MARTIN'S PATENT CULTIVATOR for breaking up stubble. These were sold by R.S. Bennetts in 1914 in 7 and 9 tined models, costing approximately £7 and £10 respectively. It required 2 or 4 horses to pull them, depending upon the model.

HIGH STREET (formerly Regent Street) showing the post office before its demolition in 1933. The Regent Cinema was built in its place.

POST OFFICE STAFF (High Street), *c.*1890. It was staffed by twenty two local people, including three telegram boys.

ST WINWOLD HORSE FAIR, held on 3 March, 8 May and 13 November, during which three days of 'merry making' ensued. In its day it was the largest horse fair in Europe, with buyers travelling from the Continent. Approximately 400 horses fetching £30-£40 each were reported to have been sold at one fair in 1914. Taken at the bottom of Bexwell Road, this is the only known picture of this event.

107 The River, Downham   Photo Raby

TIDAL RIVER, which used to transport butter to and from a large market held at Downham during the early 1800s. It was reported that in 1568 'seventeen large fishes measuring 20 to 27 feet long were caught near the bridge'. Were they sturgeon? On 31 August 1833 the bank gave way, laying waste to hundreds of acres of land. Since flooding in 1947 the banks have been heightened and strengthened.

MR MASON outside his ironmongers shop in High Street, c.1903. It was named Marchant & Mason from 1899 to the untimely death of Mr Mason in 1904.

JIM RUSSELL'S first garage along London Road, pictured in 1956 before he acquired the Vauxhall dealership during 1959.

S.T. RIX, butchers, Bridge Street, before it became a fish and chip shop. Mr Rix was paid 1d per week for advertising Charlie Chaplin's *The Kid*, playing at the Electric Cinema (Paradise Road).

RABY'S shop window display of Standard Fireworks in the 1930s.

H. BROWNE, 41 Bridge Street, *c.* 1915. Rabbits and poultry were hung out on display for sale until health regulations stopped this practice.

WILLIAM (TOM) SARGEANT on Warren's delivery cart pictured in 1919 at Stow Hall. In that year he left to start his own butcher's business in Stow Bridge.

Three

People

People make a town what it is. The following pictures show the town either at work or play and, where names are known, they have been included for added interest.

HIGH STREET decorated for King George V's Coronation in 1911.

KING GEORGE V's CORONATION, 22 June 1911. An estimated 600 teas were provided by Messrs Lyon & Son in the Market Place. As a gift, each child received a handsome Coronation mug to commemorate the occasion.

HOME GUARD SIGNAL PLATOON, 1942/43. Back row, second and third from left, are Mr Yallop and Mr Carter. Middle row, far right, is 'Tinker' Taylor. Front row, middle, is Mr H. Rose.

DOWNHAM FIRE BRIGADE drilling at their station in Paradise Road, c.1930.

INFANTS SCHOOL. A class photograph, *c*. 1910.

DOWNHAM WEDNESDAY FOOTBALL CLUB, 1938, photographed on the Howdale. Back row: -?-; J. Frost; J. Grommett; K. Elsey. Middle row: Captain Andrews; L. Wilkinson; L. Watson. Front row: ? Potter, S. Boughen; C.Hovell; J. Sargeant. The team always played matches on a Wednesday, the town's Half-day Closing.

F.WASHBY & W. CAGE's workforce posing at an unidentified building, *c.* 1920. Their yard was situated off Bexwell Road, and is still a builders yard today.

RONNIE BENNETT (front left) and farm staff at Bridge Farm, Winter 1933.

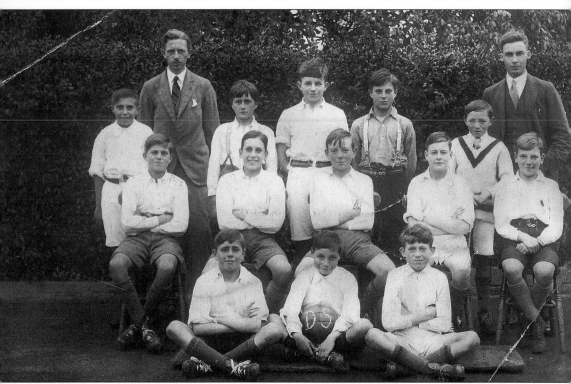

SCHOOL FOOTBALL TEAM, c. 1932. Back row: Hammond Mansell; ? Curshore; John Sparrow; Harold Rebel; ? Cauley; Lesley Watson; Jack Waterson (later headmaster). Middle row: Charle Causton; Ted Heathcote; Cliff Bond; 'Jack' Stocking; Percy Seyer. Front row: 'Stinker' Allen; Reg Dent; Len Barker.

MOTOR CYCLE RACING, Lynn Road, July 1932.

56

REMOVING THE COBBLES, 1925. No mechinical means here - just picks and shovels, with a horse-drawn cart to remove them.

FIRST WORLD WAR, showing patients recovering at the back of the National School Rooms in Howdale Road. A cut-out of Charlie Chaplin was used to raise spirits.

HOLLIES CAR PARK. It was opened in 1960 by Urban District Council Chairman and local butcher Mr C.E. Bowman (right).

MISS MAGGIE MORTON'S COMPANY presented *Two Little Drummer Boys* in the Town Hall on Wednesday 12 September 1906. The best seats cost 2s (10p) and early doors 6d (2½p) extra.

WORKERS preparing to build the Regent Cinema (1933/4).

MR CHARLES SEWTER'S FUNERAL CORTEGE, 2 MARCH 1912, proceeding down Bexwell Road. Mr Sewter was Downham Market's highly respected Police Superintendent from 1879/90.

FORESTER'S FRIENDLY SOCIETY, *c.* 1935. This group posing in Rampant Horse Lane, are preparing to take part in a parade. Mrs Parker is dressed as Maid Marion.

HOSPITAL SUNDAY, 1914. The collection raised £8 13s 6d for local hospitals.

SCHOOL TREAT, 1930. Excited children and parents wait at the station for a steam train outing to Hunstanton. This was perhaps their only trip to the sea that year.

ELEMENTARY DANCE SCHOOL, photographed during a Mount Tabor garden party at Ronnie Bennett's house, July 1932. Left to right are: Florence ?; Ellen Clarke; Flora ?; Doris Wilson; Eileen Youngs; Mary Robinson; Mrs Roberts; Eileen Warner; Mrs Alflatt; ? Barber; Rosemary ?; Gwen ?; Doreen Francis; Doris ?; Winifred Richardson; Molly ?; Gladys Fox.

CROWNING CEREMONY, *c.* 1934, on what was the Secondary School field. Dr Wales is in attendance with his frocked coat and wig (left of the carnival queen).

REVD DORMAN, Vicar of Downham Market 1924-1957 (back), Dr Wales (left) and Revd Ward (centre) posing outside the Town Hall's original main door on Bridge Street, *c.* 1930.

Four

Accidents and Incidents

'Accidents will happen', so the saying goes. Cart and bus accidents did indeed happen and some of them are recorded in this small section.

MR OZZIE RUSSELL standing beside his damaged bus in Bennett Street after causing the accident with the Crown bus. Myrtle Casey is the young lady standing opposite.

WHIT SUNDAY, 8 JUNE 1924. The Crown bus was driven by Mr Jack Savage, having been involved in an accident with Ozzie Russell's bus on its way to collect Crown Hotel customers from the train station.

PARROTT'S FIRE. The Downhams' fire engine is being used to pump water with Captain Elsey standing by.

FIRE BRIGADE IN ACTION, High Street, *c.* 1934, during a fire at Parrott's drapery shop.

MAKING SAFE, after a car has run off Cannon Square into Simpson's Cosy Cafe, *c.* 1936.

DR WALES AMBULANCE gutted by fire in the 1930s. It was housed in buildings on the site now occupied by Boots.

Five

Denver

Situated some two miles south of Downham, Denver, in 1845, was a small village including in its parish 910 inhabitants on 2,976 acres of land. It is best known for its windmill and its sluices one mile to the west of the village.

RYSTON HALL, home of the Pratt family for many hundreds of years. In 1854 it was occupied by Edward Roger Pratt and was then described as a 'handsome mansion, in a beautiful park', as it still is today.

Ketts Oak, Ryston

Photo Raby

KETTS OAK, Ryston. In Tudor times local rebels assembled by this tree before joining Ketts rebellion on Mousehold Heath, Norwich.

SLUICE ROAD, 1929. This group of children were very pleased to have their photograph taken. If one was to stand here today, one would risk life and limb.

THE CARPENTERS ARMS public house (1917) was converted into a private home a few years ago.

THE CLUB HOUSE, RYSTON, *c.*1934. It has been extended and is today Ryston Golf Club's headquarters.

THE ROUND HOUSE, Ryston, 1915, pictured with a thatched roof. It is believed that a spark from a passing traction engine destroyed the roof.

The New Jubilee Hall, Denver.

NEW JUBILEE HALL, Wincommon Road. Erected in 1935, this wooden building was the village hall until a fire destroyed it in 1951.

45   Sluice Road, Denver

Photo Raby

SLUICE ROAD, 1934. It is basically the same today, except the shop has been converted into a private dwelling. Today, Denver Garage showroom stands where the brick wall is.

SLUICE ROAD, *c.* 1930. Captain George Manby, was born at Easthall Manor in 1765 pictured on the extreme left. He was an eccentric inventor of an apparatus called the 'Breeches Buoy', a portable fire extinguisher, and many other life-saving devices.

MILL AND COMMON. Until about the late '60s early '70s, cattle were allowed to roam free, causing accidents and many near-misses to traffic heading down to Denver Sluice.

DENVER SLUICE, c.1922. A sluice was first constructed on this site in 1651. Collapsing 64 years later, in 1713, it was rebuilt in 1750. The present sluice and lock were designed and constructed by John Rennie in 1834 at a cost of £30,000. Before the Flood Relief Channel was dug in 1959, a road led to the sluice where Denver Yacht Clubhouse now stands.

DENVER SLUICE; 1924 saw a new larger gate added plus various other improvements. During this work, vehicles had to travel via Ten Mile Bank. Pedestrians could cross over the river by a footbridge (foreground).

DENVER MILL, *c.* 1920. Built in 1835, Denver Mill only ceased to be wind operated in 1941. Milling continued under diesel power until the death of Mr Thomas Harris in 1969. The pit today is only a shadow of its former self.

FISHING COTTAGE (*c.*1924) with a boathouse fronting the River Great Ouse. With a need to increase the flow of flood water from the River Wissey (right of the house) the bank was cut back, requiring the removal of all trees and buildings, some over 40 years old.

74

Six
Hilgay

Four miles south of Downham on the main London road, Hilgay parish had in 1852, 1,710 inhabitants in 395 houses. Mr W.L. Jones and Mrs Peel were owners of the 7,583 acres of land on which Hilgay stood, half of which was fen. The two hundred allotments containing 102 acres are supposed to have been awarded in the reign of Charles II for use by the poor. Many trades were present including doctor baker and blacksmith. Six pubs (the Bell, Dog & Duck, George & Dragon, White Swan, Jolly Angler, Rose & Crown) and four beer houses gave a focus for village life.

"Snore Hall" Fordham.   Photo: Raby.

SNORE HALL, c. 1930, one of England's oldest country houses. When King Charles was on the run from the Roundheads in 1646 a change of horse and clothing were provided by Ralph Skipworth at Snore Hall.

10,119 The Causeway, Hilgay

THE CAUSEWAY, 1938, looking towards Denver. Snore Hall stands on rising ground to the right. The Flood Relief Channel, dug during the 1970s, now runs across near the second bend. A10 road improvements required straightening the road and uprooting almost all trees.

BRIDGE HOUSE, 1914. Before the A10 road improvements in 1980 the old road out of Hilgay to Downham led off to the right.

THE RIVER WISSEY helps with draining the fenlands. It was used mainly from 1925 to transport sugar beet upstream to the then-new sugar processing factory at Wissington. With improved roads this ceased in the 1950s. 'Faggots' stacked on the bank would be used for bank strengthening.

BRIDGE STREET, *c.* 1915, with a dirt track for a main road. Every person here took time to stop and face the camera.

BRIDGE STREET, *c.* 1955. The same view some 40 years later but with Dent's garage pumps, white lines, television aerials and telephone cables apparent. Mr Veal's cows are being driven through the village to be milked.

Archdeacon of Wisbech, George Ward, and
his wife. He was Rector of Hilgay until 1947.

THE RECTORY as it was in 1929. Many large garden fetes were held on the spacious lawns.
The last vicar to live here was Revd J. Beloe.

FANCY DRESS COMPETITION, 1935, includes B. Spinks; B. Kisby; Joyce Veal; Daphne Crane; Ronnie Armsby; V. Holman and Mr Brundle.

FANCY DRESS COMPETITION, 1934, from left to right: L .Holman; A. Everritt; M.Barrett; G. Stokes; T. Spinks; L. Boyce; H. Taylor; L. Armsby; ? Ferguson; N. Ferguson. Front row: M. Palmer, ? Dent; ? Lane with R. Dent dressed as the pirate and B. Spinks as the warrior.

WOODHALL, the home of the Stocks farming family.

ROSE COTTAGE, *c.* 1920. An idyllic rose-covered cottage in Hubbard Drove with the Rectory behind.

NEW SCHOOL, 1907. The building was extended with the addition of a kitchen in 1911.

HILGAY FOOTBALL TEAM, *c.* 1934. Back row: F. Everritt (goal keeper). Front row, left: L. Thornton. Middle: ? Cross and C. Horton (right).

HIGH STREET, 1915, showing The Swan and The George & Dragon pubs. As the latter stuck out onto the road it was struck on numerous occasions when large aircraft wings were transported through Hilgay in the late 1950s. All the cottages and The George & Dragon were demolished to improve traffic flow through the village around 1961.

WESLEYAN SUNDAY SCHOOL, The commemerative stone is being laid by Mr Albert Coulson, post master, on 11 September, 1912.

THE PITTS, *c.* 1910. Situated on the main road through the village, Mr Smith, the farrier, is here showing one of his horses. Visible above the cottages on the left are sails from a windmill which blew down in a gale in the 1920s. The families Mann, Harnwell and Cox lived in the cottages on the right.

GEORGE WHITTOME'S premises in Holts Lane. This business was started by George during the late 1800s. Upon his death, his son Fred took over until its closure in the 1950s. The family also owned one of the two windmills in Hilgay.

LONDON ROAD, *c.*1915 showing Miss Moorfoot and her sister standing at their front door (left). After their death in the late 1940s the house was bought by a local character, Mr 'Funny' Carnell.

HOLTS LANE, 1906. This badly faded photograph shows half the lane. These two-up, two-down cottages were demolished when they became sub-standard.

SILVER JUBILEE, 1935. Mrs Rolfe; Mrs Doy; Mrs Bland; Mrs Horton; Mrs Spinks and Mrs Katie Doy are preparing for celebrations in the village hall.

BANK REPAIRS being carried out by D. Bland; H. Everritt; L. Doy; A. Eagle and S. Thurlow.

PRIMITIVE CHAPEL, 1910, London Road. It ceased to be a chapel in 1938 and was used as a school canteen during the war. It finally became Law's cycle shop in the early 1950s and was demolished in 1995.

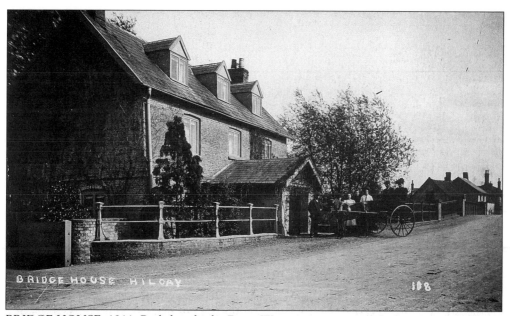

BRIDGE HOUSE, 1911. Built beside the River Wissey, it was owned at this time by a farmer, Mr Thompson. It became the Cross Keys Hotel in about 1982.

WAR MEMORIAL. Situated on the junction of High Street and Church Road, it was dedicated in 1921 to the memory of those who lost their lives in the First World War.

STOCKS HILL, 1930, showing, left to right: Bill Spink's shoe repair shop, Miss Emily Anderson's sweet and tobacco shop, The Swan public house and Dent's butchers shop.

CHURCH AVENUE as it looked in 1923.

EAST END, 1906. Unfortunately, the picture is very badly faded. Standing on this site now is a row of new modern houses overlooking the River Wissey.

HIGH STREET, 1914, showing two shops: Mrs Firman's bakery and a sweet and grocery shop run by Miss B. Dent.

HILGAY EXCELSIOR BAND, c.1936, including drummer B. Everritt, with J. Frost and C. Laws. This band formed around 1896 and is still in existence today as Hilgay Silver Band.

Seven

Southery

Southery is described in a Norfolk directory of 1845 as 'a considerable village, on the London Road 7 miles south of Downham, on a gentle eminence surrounded by fens and marshes'. Nowadays the marshes have been drained and the village bypassed. It is still a considerable village. With many new houses, the inhabitants have increased greatly from 739 in 1831.

WESLEYAN CHAPEL and cottages, 1906. The chapel was built in 1842. It was replaced in 1990 with a new purpose-built chapel. A boot repairers business is advertised over the door of the right hand side cottage.

A 1911 postcard showing how they propose to pass the time at Southery.

SOUTHERY MANOR HOUSE.

SOUTHERY MANOR, 1913. It stood on Victory Corner until its demolition in 1963.

WESTGATE STREET, 1906, looking into Southery with the Manor House on the left.

OLD CHURCH and WINDMILL, *c.*1915. This listed building is believed to have been built in the fourteenth century. Following its demise as a place of worship, it became overgrown with ivy and was completely removed ten to twelve years ago. The postmill was pulled down in 1929, by Mr Ronnie Palmer using his steam engine attached to a wire rope.

NEW CHURCH. The foundation stone was laid on 7 September 1858 by Mr John Thomas, Lord Bishop of Norwich with the church being dedicated to St Mary the Virgin. The Revd A.E. Julius was the rector.

94

THE WAREING, 1908. A tranquil scene with a farmer soaking his cart wheels. This expanded the joints and stopped them from squeaking. Situated opposite Feltwell Road, The Wareing was filled in during the late 1950s. Southery village sign now stands here.

UPGATE STREET as it appeared in the late 1920s. The Wareing was situated in the trees pictured at the top of the hill.

THE FLOODS, Winter 1947, looking out of Southery with Sedge Fen on the left and the pumping engine behind the trees. Floods had covered the main road by several inches.

THE 1947 FLOODS. Low lying farms and hundreds of acres of prime farm land were soon under water once the bank broke.